SCHOLASTIC

Writing Lessons to Meet the Common Core

Grade 3

Linda Ward Beech

NEW YORK • TORONTO • LONDON • AUCKLAND • SYDNEY
MEXICO CITY • NEW DELHI • HONG KONG • BUENOS AIRES

Teaching Resources

Cover design by Scott Davis
Interior design by Kathy Massaro
Illustrations by Maxie Chambliss, Rusty Fletcher, Anne Kennedy, and Sydney Wright

ISBN: 978-0-545-39162-7

2   3   4   5   6   7   8   9   10   40   20   19   18   17   16   15   14   13

Contents

Opinion Writing Lessons

Informative/Explanatory Writing Lessons

Narrative Writing Lessons

Student Assessment Checklists

About This Book

. . . .

To build a foundation for college and career readiness, students need to learn to use writing as a way of offering and supporting opinions, demonstrating understanding of the subjects they are studying, and conveying real and imagined experiences and events. They learn to appreciate that a key purpose of writing is to communicate clearly to an external, sometimes unfamiliar audience, and they begin to adapt the form and content of their writing to accomplish a particular task and purpose.

—COMMON CORE STATE STANDARDS FOR ENGLISH LANGUAGE ARTS, JUNE 2010

This book includes step-by-step instructions for teaching the three forms of writing—Opinion, Informative/Explanatory, and Narrative—covered in the Common Core State Standards (CCSS). The CCSS are a result of a state-led effort to establish a single set of clear educational standards aimed at providing students nationwide with a high-quality education. The standards outline the knowledge and skills that students should achieve during their years in school.

The writing standards are a subset of the Common Core English Language Arts Standards. They provide "a focus for instruction" to help students gain a mastery of a range of skills and applications necessary for writing clear prose. This book is divided into three main sections; each section includes six lessons devoted to one of the writing forms covered in the CCSS for grade 3. You'll find more about each of these types of writing on pages 6–7.

- **Lessons 1–6** (pages 8–25) focus on the standards for writing opinion pieces.
- **Lessons 7–12** (pages 26–43) emphasize standards particular to informative/explanatory writing.
- **Lessons 13–18** (pages 44–61) address the standards for narrative writing.

Although the CCSS do not specify how to teach any form of writing, the lessons in this book follow the gradual release of responsibility model of instruction: I Do It, We Do It, You Do It (Pearson & Gallagher, 1983). This model provides educators with a framework for releasing responsibility to students in a gradual manner. It recognizes that we learn best when a concept is demonstrated to us; when we have sufficient time to practice it with support; and when we are then given the opportunity to try it on our own. Each phase is equally important, but the chief goal is to teach for independence—the You Do It phase—so that students really learn to take over the skill and apply it in new situations.

....

Pearson, P. D., & Gallagher, M. C. (1983). "The Instruction of Reading Comprehension." *Contemporary Educational Psychology*, 8 (3).

A Look at the Lessons

The lessons in each section progress in difficulty and increase in the number of objectives and standards covered. This format enables you to use beginning or later lessons in a section depending on your students' abilities. Each lesson begins with a list of the objectives and standards included. A general reproducible assessment checklist of standards for each writing form appears at the end of the book. (See pages 62–64.)

Here's a look at the features in each lesson.

Lesson Page 1

The first page is the teaching page of each lesson. It provides a step-by-step plan for using the student reproducible on the second lesson page and the On Your Own activity on the third lesson page. The teaching page closely follows the organization of the student reproducibles. This page also models sample text that students might generate when completing page 2 of the lesson. Finally, the teaching page includes an opportunity for students to review their classmates' work using the reproducible assessment checklist customized to the lesson's writing form. Each checklist also reminds students to check for correct punctuation, spelling, and paragraph form.

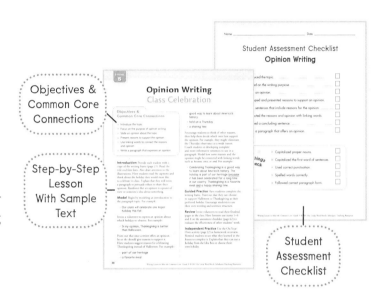

Objectives & Common Core Connections

Step-by-Step Lesson With Sample Text

Student Assessment Checklist

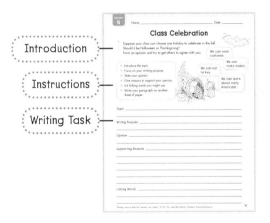

Introduction

Instructions

Writing Task

Lesson Page 2

The second page is a student reproducible, which is the core of the lesson. Students complete this writing frame as you guide them. In most lessons, students use the completed page as the basis for a paragraph they write on a separate sheet of paper.

Although you provide a model for completing this reproducible, you'll want to encourage students to use their own ideas, words, and sentences as much as possible.

Lesson Page 3

The third page is a writing frame for independent work. It follows a format similar to the one students used for the first reproducible. Students choose their topic from the suggested list or use their own idea for the topic. In most lessons, students use the completed page as the basis for a paragraph they write on a separate sheet of paper.

Introduction

Topic Suggestions

Writing Task

Three Forms of Writing

The CCSS focus on three forms of writing—opinion, informative/explanatory, and narrative.

Opinion Pieces (Standards W.3.1a, W.3.1b, W.3.1c, W.3.1d)

The purpose of writing opinion pieces is to convince others to think or act in a certain way, to encourage readers or listeners to share the writer's point of view, beliefs, or position. Opinion pieces are also known as persuasive writing.

> I think it would be a lot of fun to climb this tree.

In developing an opinion piece, students must learn to introduce the topic, present a point of view, and supply valid reasons, facts, and expert opinions to support it. Phrases such as *I think, I believe, you should/should not* all signal persuasive writing.

> You should not miss reading this book.

When teaching these lessons, display different examples of opinion pieces. You might include:

- editorials
- book, movie, TV, and theater reviews
- print advertisements
- letters to the editor
- feature columns

> As students learn to produce different forms of writing, they are also enhancing their ability to recognize these forms in their reading.

Informative/Explanatory Writing (Standards W.3.2a, W.3.2b, W.3.2c, W.3.2d)

The purpose of informative/explanatory writing is to inform the reader by giving facts, explanations, and other information. Informative/explanatory writing is also called expository writing.

When writing an informative/explanatory piece, students must introduce the topic and give facts, details, descriptions, and other information about the topic. The information should also be organized in a logical way. Many kinds of informative/explanatory writing require research. Sometimes illustrations are included with informative/explanatory pieces.

> You can make a rain gauge to measure rainfall.

> A hammock is a hanging bed used for sleeping or relaxing.

Display different examples of informative/explanatory writing. You might include:

- reports
- news articles
- how-to articles
- biographies
- directions
- textbooks
- magazines
- recipes

Writing Lessons to Meet the Common Core: Grade 3 © 2013 by Linda Ward Beech, Scholastic Teaching Resources

Narrative Writing (Standards W.3.3a, W.3.3b, W.3.3c, W.3.3d)

The purpose of narrative writing is to entertain. A narrative gives an account or a story. Usually, a narrative tells about something that happens over a period of time. Narratives can be true or imaginary.

Suddenly, they were really flying, soaring in the cool, clear air.

When working on a narrative, students must develop a real or imagined experience or event. They must also establish a situation or plot, create characters, and recount events in a chronological sequence. Narratives usually include descriptive details. Many include dialogue.

You sold me socks that don't match!

That's impossible!

When introducing narrative writing, display different examples. You might include:

- stories
- mysteries
- fables
- fairy tales
- folktales
- science fiction
- friendly letters

Additional Writing Standards

Although this book focuses on the forms of writing called for in the CCSS, you can also incorporate the standards that relate to the production and distribution of writing and research to build and present knowledge. These standards include:

- W.3.4 Produce writing in which the development and organization are appropriate to task and purpose.

- W.3.5 Develop and strengthen writing as needed by planning, revising, and editing.

- W.3.6 Use keyboard skills to produce and publish writing.

- W.3.7 Conduct short research projects to build knowledge about a topic.

- W.3.8 Recall information from experiences and gather information from print and digital sources.

- W.3.10 Write routinely over extended time and shorter time frames (allowing time for research, reflection, and revision) for a range of tasks, purposes, and audiences.

Language Standards

In addition, you can incorporate the CCSS Language Standards that focus on the conventions of standard English grammar and usage when writing or speaking (L.3.1); the conventions of standard English capitalization, punctuation, and spelling when writing (L.3.2); and the knowledge of language conventions when writing, speaking, reading, or listening (L.3.3).

Writing Lessons to Meet the Common Core: Grade 3 © 2013 by Linda Ward Beech, Scholastic Teaching Resources

Opinion Writing
Something New

* Introduce the topic.
* Focus on the purpose of opinion writing.
* State an opinion about the topic.
* Develop a list of reasons to support the opinion.
* Write sentences that include reasons for the opinion.

Introduction Provide each student with a copy of the writing frame (page 9). Read the title and first lines. Also draw attention to the illustration. Have volunteers read the captions. Invite students to think of other things they might say about a T-shirt they created. Tell students that they will be writing to persuade other people to share their opinion about it. Explain that an opinion is a point of view or someone's idea about something.

Model Tell students that in an opinion piece writers should introduce the topic. Write the topic in sentence form on the board. For example:

* I designed a new T-shirt.

Invite a volunteer to suggest what the designer's opinion about the T-shirt might be. For example:

* I think this is a terrific T-shirt.

Remind students that they are writing to persuade their readers to agree with them about the T-shirt. Ask: *How do you persuade someone to agree with you?* Help students understand that a writer might give reasons to support an opinion.

For example:

* it's unusual
* it's comfortable
* it's original
* it fits well

Encourage students to come up with other reasons, then talk about the different reasons and how they might be useful in persuading someone to think the T-shirt is cool. Coach students in developing some practice sentences based on the reasons. For example:

* I like the shirt because it's unusual.

Guided Practice Have students complete the writing frame. As an option, you might have them draw their own versions of a new T-shirt and write about that. Instruct them to introduce the topic, state an opinion, focus on the purpose of writing about the topic, and list reasons to support the opinion. Encourage students to use their own words and sentence structure.

Review Invite volunteers to read their finished pages to the class. Have listeners use items 1–5 on the assessment checklist (page 62) to evaluate the effectiveness of other students' work.

Independent Practice Use the On Your Own activity (page 10) as homework or review. Encourage students to use what they learned in the lesson to complete the page. Explain that they can choose a topic from the Idea Box or use their own idea. Provide paper so students can draw a picture of their design before they begin writing about it.

Writing Lessons to Meet the Common Core: Grade 3 © 2013 by Linda Ward Beech, Scholastic Teaching Resources

Something New

Suppose you design a new T-shirt.
You think it's great.
How can you get others to agree with you?

It's new.

It's different.

It's cool!

- Introduce the topic.
- Focus on your writing purpose.
- State your opinion.
- List reasons to support your opinion.
- Write some practice sentences.

Topic _____

Writing Purpose _____

_____

Opinion _____

_____

Supporting Reasons _____

_____

_____

_____

Practice Sentences _____

_____

_____

_____

_____

_____

On Your Own

Pretend you are a great designer. Choose a design topic from the Idea Box or think of one of your own. Draw a picture of your design. Then, complete this page to persuade others to agree that your design is great.

Idea Box

○ New Cereal Box   ○ My Idea: _____

○ New Video Game   _____

○ New Bike   _____

Topic _____

Writing Purpose _____

_____

Opinion _____

_____

Supporting Reasons _____

_____

_____

_____

Sentences _____

_____

_____

_____

_____

_____

Opinion Writing
Climb or Not?

Objectives & Common Core Connections

* Introduce the topic.
* Focus on the purpose of opinion writing.
* State an opinion about the topic.
* Develop a list of reasons to support the opinion.
* Write sentences that include reasons for the opinion.

Introduction Provide each student with a copy of the writing frame (page 12). Read the title and first lines. Also draw attention to the tree in the picture and the captions. Encourage students to think about other things they might say about the tree. Tell them that they will be writing to persuade other people to share their opinion about climbing the tree. Remind students that an opinion is a point of view or someone's idea about something.

Model Tell students that in an opinion piece writers should introduce the topic. Write a topic in sentence form on the board. For example:

* Some people like to climb trees.

Invite a volunteer to tell you what his or her opinion is. For example:

* I think it would be a lot of fun to climb this tree.

Remind students that they are writing to persuade their readers to agree with them about climbing the tree. Ask: *How do you persuade someone to agree with you?* Help students understand that a writer might give reasons to support an opinion. For example:

* would be a challenge
* could pick an apple
* view would be great
* could be a secret hiding place

Ask students to come up with other reasons for climbing the tree, then talk about these reasons and how they might be useful in persuading someone to climb the tree. Work with students to determine which reasons best support the opinion. For example, students might eliminate the second reason because not all trees have apples. Coach students in developing practice sentences based on the reasons. For example:

* Climbing the tree would be a good challenge.

Guided Practice Have students complete the writing frame. Instruct them to introduce the topic, focus on the purpose of writing, state an opinion, and list reasons to support their opinion. Encourage students to use their own wording and sentence structure. Point out that they can state a different opinion and use different reasons to support it.

Review Invite volunteers to read their finished pages to the class. Have listeners use items 1–5 on the assessment checklist (page 62) to evaluate the effectiveness of other students' work.

Independent Practice Use the On Your Own activity (page 13) as homework or review. Encourage students to use what they learned in the lesson to complete the page. Explain that they can choose a topic from the Idea Box or use their own idea.

Climb or Not?

Should you and your friends climb this tree?
Form an opinion.
Then, try to get others to agree with you.

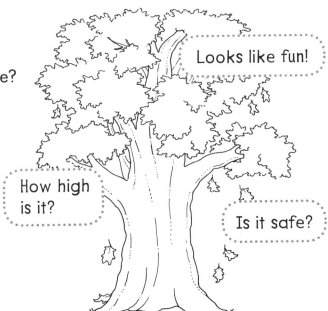

- Introduce the topic.
- Focus on your writing purpose.
- State your opinion.
- List reasons to support your opinion.
- Write some practice sentences.

Topic _____

Writing Purpose _____

_____

Opinion _____

_____

Supporting Reasons _____

_____

_____

_____

Practice Sentences _____

_____

_____

_____

_____

_____

On Your Own

Choose a daring activity from the Idea Box or think of one of your own. Form an opinion about the safety of the activity. Complete this page to persuade others to agree with you.

Idea Box

○ Jumping From One Huge Boulder to Another

○ Swinging on a Vine on a Tree

○ Walking on a Log Across a Stream

○ My Idea: _____

_____

Topic _____

Writing Purpose _____

_____

Opinion _____

_____

Supporting Reasons _____

_____

_____

_____

Sentences _____

_____

_____

_____

_____

_____

Opinion Writing
Where to Go

Objectives & Common Core Connections

* Introduce the topic.
* Focus on the purpose of opinion writing.
* State an opinion about the topic.
* Present reasons to support the opinion.
* Write a paragraph that expresses an opinion.

Introduction Provide each student with a copy of the writing frame (page 15). Read the title and first lines. Also draw attention to the illustrations. Have volunteers read the captions. Ask students to think about which field trip—the zoo or the dinosaur museum—they think would be best. Explain that they will be writing a paragraph to persuade others to share their opinion. Reinforce that an opinion is a point of view or someone's idea about something.

Model Review that a paragraph is a group of sentences about the same idea or topic. Tell students that they should introduce the topic. Write the topic in sentence form on the board. For example:

* Where should our class go on a field trip?

Focus students on the purpose of opinion writing: to persuade others to agree with their opinion. Invite a volunteer to give you his or her opinion about where to go. For example:

* A visit to the zoo would be very exciting.

Point out that once a writer offers an opinion, he or she should give reasons to support it. Ask students to suggest reasons to support the opinion in the example. For example:

* see wild animals up close
* compare different animals
* learn a lot by observing the animals
* fun to watch the baby animals play
* talk to the animals

Encourage students to come up with other reasons, then work with them to determine which reasons best support the opinion. For example, talking to the animals might be less compelling than other reasons. Coach students in developing complete sentences to use in the paragraph. For example:

* The zoo has wild animals that we can view up close. We can learn a lot by observing these animals. We can also compare different animals. It's fun to watch the baby animals play.

Guided Practice Have students complete the writing frame. Point out that they can choose either the zoo or the dinosaur museum as their topic. Encourage students to use their own words and sentence structure.

Review Invite volunteers to read their finished pages to the class. Have listeners use items 1–5 and 8 on the assessment checklist (page 62) to evaluate the effectiveness of other students' work.

Independent Practice Use the On Your Own activity (page 16) as homework or review. Remind students to use what they learned in the lesson to complete the page. Explain that they can choose a topic from the Idea Box or use their own idea.

Name _____ Date _____

Where to Go

We can see elephants.

⭐ Your class is going on a field trip.
Should you go to the zoo or to the dinosaur museum?
Form an opinion and try to get others to agree with you.

- Introduce the topic.
- Focus on your writing purpose.
- State your opinion.
- Give reasons to support your opinion.
- Write your paragraph.

We can find out how dinosaurs might have looked.

Topic _____

Writing Purpose _____

_____

Opinion _____

_____

Supporting Reasons _____

_____

_____

_____

Paragraph _____

_____

_____

_____

_____

_____

Name _____ Date _____

On Your Own

Choose a place for an end-of-year class trip from the Idea Box or think of one of your own. Form an opinion about the place. Complete this page to persuade others to agree with you.

Idea Box

○ Fair   ○ Beach   ○ Park   ○ My Idea:

PARK

_____

_____

Topic _____

Writing Purpose _____

_____

Opinion _____

_____

Supporting Reasons _____

_____

_____

_____

Paragraph _____

_____

_____

_____

_____

_____

_____

Opinion Writing
A Must-Read Book

Objectives & Common Core Connections

* Introduce the topic.
* Focus on the purpose of opinion writing.
* State an opinion about the topic.
* Present reasons to support the opinion.
* Write a paragraph that expresses an opinion.

Introduction Provide each student with a copy of the writing frame (page 18). Read the title and first lines. Some students will be familiar with the book. Have a copy on hand to read aloud to the class. Explain that students will be writing a paragraph to persuade others to read the book. Reinforce that an opinion is a point of view or someone's idea about something.

Model Tell students that they will begin by writing an introduction to the topic. Write a sample introductory sentence on the board. For example:

* *Sarah, Plain and Tall* is a book by Patricia MacLachlan.

Invite a volunteer to offer an opinion about the book. For example:

* You should not miss reading this book.

Point out that once a writer offers an opinion, he or she should give reasons to support it. Ask students to suggest reasons to support the opinion in the example. For example:

* characters seem real
* learn about the past
* has a cat in it
* sad and happy story
* good ending

Encourage students to think of other reasons, then work with them to decide which reasons best support the opinion. For example, not all students will think having a cat in the story is a good reason. Coach students in developing complete sentences to use in a paragraph. For example:

* The characters and feelings in the story seem real. The book also helps you learn about the past. This book keeps you reading because it has sad parts and happy ones, too. It has a very good ending.

Guided Practice Have students complete the writing frame. Encourage them to use their own words and sentence structure.

Review Invite volunteers to read their finished pages to the class. Have listeners use items 1–5 and 8 on the assessment checklist (page 62) to evaluate the effectiveness of other students' work.

Independent Practice Use the On Your Own activity (page 19) as homework or review. Remind students to use what they learned in the lesson to complete the page. Explain that they can choose a book from the Idea Box or use a book of their choice.

A Must-Read Book

You have read a book called *Sarah, Plain and Tall* by Patricia MacLachlan.
You want your friends to read it, too.
You need to persuade them.

- Introduce the topic.
- Focus on your writing purpose.
- State your opinion.
- List reasons to support your opinion.
- Write your paragraph.

Topic _____

Writing Purpose _____

_____

Opinion _____

_____

Supporting Reasons _____

_____

_____

_____

Paragraph _____

_____

_____

_____

_____

_____

Writing Lessons to Meet the Common Core: Grade 3 © 2013 by Linda Ward Beech, Scholastic Teaching Resources

On Your Own

Choose one of the books from the Idea Box or pick another book you have read that you think others should read, too. Complete this page to persuade them.

Idea Box

○ *Bunicula* by Deborah and James Howe

○ *The Josefina Quilt Story* by Eleanor Coerr

○ *Stone Fox* by John Reynolds Gardiner

○ My Book: _____

_____

Topic _____

Writing Purpose _____

_____

Opinion _____

_____

Supporting Reasons _____

_____

_____

_____

Paragraph _____

_____

_____

_____

_____

_____

Opinion Writing
Class Celebration

Objectives & Common Core Connections

* Introduce the topic.
* Focus on the purpose of opinion writing.
* State an opinion about the topic.
* Present reasons to support the opinion.
* Use linking words to connect the reasons and opinion.
* Write a paragraph that expresses an opinion.

Introduction Provide each student with a copy of the writing frame (page 21). Read the title and first lines. Also draw attention to the illustrations. Have students read the captions and think about the holiday they would most like to celebrate in class. Explain that they will write a paragraph to persuade others to share their opinion. Reinforce that an opinion is a point of view or someone's idea about something.

Model Begin by modeling an introduction to the paragraph topic. For example:

* Our class will celebrate one major holiday this fall.

Invite a volunteer to express an opinion about which holiday to observe. For example:

* In my opinion, Thanksgiving is better than Halloween.

Point out that once a writer offers an opinion, he or she should give reasons to support it. Have students suggest reasons for celebrating Thanksgiving instead of Halloween. For example:

* part of our heritage
* a favorite meal

* good way to learn about America's history
* held on a Thursday
* a sharing time

Encourage students to think of other reasons, then help them decide which ones best support the opinion. For example, they might eliminate the Thursday observance as a weak reason. Coach students in developing complete and more informative sentences to use in a paragraph. Model how some reasons and the opinion might be connected with linking words such as *because, since,* or *and.* For example:

* Celebrating Thanksgiving is a good way to learn about America's history. The holiday is part of our heritage <u>because</u> it has been celebrated for a long time in our country. Thanksgiving is a favorite meal <u>and</u> a happy sharing time.

Guided Practice Have students complete the writing frame. Point out that they can choose to support Halloween or Thanksgiving as their preferred holiday. Encourage students to use their own wording and sentence structure.

Review Invite volunteers to read their finished pages to the class. Have listeners use items 1–6 and 8 on the assessment checklist (page 62) to evaluate the effectiveness of other students' work.

Independent Practice Use the On Your Own activity (page 22) as homework or review. Remind students to use what they learned in the lesson to complete it. Explain that they can use a holiday from the Idea Box or choose their own holiday.

Class Celebration

Suppose your class can choose one holiday to celebrate in the fall.
Should it be Halloween or Thanksgiving?
Form an opinion and try to get others to agree with you.

We can wear costumes.

We can make masks.

We can eat turkey.

We can learn about early Americans.

- Introduce the topic.
- Focus on your writing purpose.
- State your opinion.
- Give reasons to support your opinion.
- List linking words you might use.
- Write your paragraph on another sheet of paper.

Topic _____

_____

Writing Purpose _____

_____

Opinion _____

_____

Supporting Reasons _____

_____

_____

_____

_____

_____

Linking Words _____

_____

On Your Own

Choose one of the holidays from the Idea Box that you would like your class to celebrate, or think of another holiday. Complete this page. Then, write a paragraph on another sheet of paper to persuade others to agree with you.

Idea Box

○ Valentine's Day

○ Presidents' Day

○ Earth Day

○ My Idea: _____ _____

Topic _____
_____

Writing Purpose _____
_____

Opinion _____
_____

Supporting Reasons _____
_____
_____
_____
_____

Linking Words _____
_____

Opinion Writing
Our Mascot

Objectives & Common Core Connections

* Introduce the topic.
* Focus on the purpose of opinion writing.
* State an opinion about the topic.
* Present reasons to support the opinion.
* Use linking words to connect the reasons and opinion.
* Provide a concluding statement.
* Write a paragraph that expresses an opinion.

Introduction Provide each student with a copy of the writing frame (page 24). Have students read the title and first lines. Also draw attention to the illustrations and captions. Ask students to think about which mascot—the butterfly or parrot—they think the class should have. Explain that they will be writing a paragraph to persuade others to agree with their opinion.

Model Begin by modeling an introduction and opinion for the paragraph. For example:

* The students in our class want to have a mascot. I think a parrot would be an excellent choice.

Invite volunteers to offer reasons to support this opinion. For example:

* colorful feathers
* responds to people
* has claws
* can imitate sounds
* repeats words and sentences

Encourage students to think of other reasons, then work with them to decide which ones best support the opinion. For example, students might eliminate claws as a weak reason. Coach them in developing complete and more informative sentences to use in a paragraph. Model how some reasons and the opinion can be connected with linking words, such as *also*, *because*, or *since*. For example:

* The colorful feathers of a parrot would make it cheerful to have around. Also, a parrot responds to people. It can imitate sounds. It can repeat words and sentences that people say.

Tell students that a good persuasive paragraph usually has a concluding sentence. This sentence restates the writer's opinion. For example:

* Because it communicates well, a parrot would be a good mascot for our class.

Guided Practice Have students complete the writing frame. Point out that they can choose to support the butterfly or the parrot as a class mascot. Encourage students to use their own wording and sentence structure.

Review Invite volunteers to read their finished pages to the class. Have listeners use items 1–8 on the assessment checklist (page 62) to evaluate the effectiveness of other students' work.

Independent Practice Use the On Your Own activity (page 25) as homework or review. Remind students to use what they learned in the lesson to complete it. Explain that they can choose a school mascot from the Idea Box or use their own idea.

Name _____ Date _____

Our Mascot

Suppose your class is going to pick a mascot
(a good luck animal).
Should it be a parrot or a butterfly?
Form an opinion and try to get others to agree with you.

very smart

popular bird

- Introduce the topic and focus on your writing purpose.
- State your opinion and give reasons to support it.
- List linking words you might use.
- Include a concluding sentence.
- Write your paragraph on another sheet of paper.

beautiful wings

interesting
life cycle

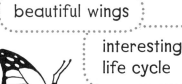

Topic _____

_____

Writing Purpose _____

_____

Opinion _____

_____

Supporting Reasons _____

_____

_____

_____

_____

Linking Words _____

_____

Concluding Sentence _____

_____

Writing Lessons to Meet the Common Core: Grade 3 © 2013 by Linda Ward Beech, Scholastic Teaching Resources

Name _____ Date _____

On Your Own

Choose one of the animals from the Idea Box that you would like for a school mascot, or think of another animal. Complete this page. Then, write a paragraph on another sheet of paper to persuade others to agree with you.

Idea Box

○ Gorilla   ○ Kangaroo   ○ Elephant   ○ My Idea: _____

Topic _____

Writing Purpose _____

Opinion _____

Supporting Reasons _____

_____

_____

_____

Linking Words _____

_____

Concluding Sentence _____

_____

Informative Writing
Wind at Work

Objectives & Common Core Connections

* Introduce the topic.
* Focus on the purpose of informative writing.
* Develop information about the topic.
* Group and organize information to make the topic clear.

Introduction Provide each student with a copy of the writing frame (page 27). Read the title and first lines. Also point out the pictures. Discuss the purpose of informative writing. Make sure students understand that the purpose is to inform the reader.

Model You might say: *The pictures show things that the wind can move. That's the topic I will write about. So my introduction might be:*

* The wind can make many things move.

Explain that the next step is to develop information about the topic. Ask: *Would the wind affect all the items in the same way?* Write students' ideas on the board. For example, the wind might:

* roll the tennis ball
* float the feather in the air
* ring the chimes
* bang the shutter
* wave the flag

Explain that a writer organizes or groups information about a topic to make it easier for a reader to understand. Have students suggest how they might group the ways the wind affects the items. For example: In the first group of sentences below, the wind causes different kinds of motion; in the second group, the wind causes movement and sounds.

* The wind moves a tennis ball by making it roll.
* The wind makes a feather float in the air.
* A flag waves when the wind moves it.

* When the wind moves chimes, they ring.
* The wind can move a shutter and cause it to bang.

Guided Practice Have students complete the writing frame. Encourage them to use their own words and sentence structure when they group their ideas.

Review Invite volunteers to read their finished pages to the class. Have listeners use items 1–3 and 6 on the assessment checklist (page 63) to evaluate the effectiveness of other students' work.

Independent Practice Use the On Your Own activity (page 28) as homework or review. Encourage students to use what they learned in the lesson to complete the page. Explain that they can choose a topic from the Idea Box or use their own idea.

Name _____ Date _____

Wind at Work

Here comes the wind!
What can it do to these things?

- Introduce the topic.
- Focus on your writing purpose.
- Tell what the wind can do to the things in the pictures.
- Group the information.

Topic _____

Writing Purpose _____

Information _____

_____

_____

_____

_____

Group the Information

Movement _____

_____

_____

_____

Movement and Sound _____

_____

_____

_____

On Your Own

Choose a weather topic from the Idea Box or think of one your own. Tell what this kind of weather can do. Complete the page.

Idea Box

○ Rain   ○ Sun   ○ Snow   ○ My Idea:

_____

_____

Topic _____

Writing Purpose _____

_____

Information _____

_____

_____

_____

_____

_____

Group the Information

First Group _____

_____

_____

_____

Second Group _____

_____

_____

Writing Lessons to Meet the Common Core: Grade 3 © 2013 by Linda Ward Beech, Scholastic Teaching Resources

Informative Writing
Here's a Hammock

Objectives & Common Core Connections

* Introduce the topic.
* Focus on the purpose of informative writing.
* Develop information about the topic.
* Use facts to tell about the topic.
* Group and organize information to make the topic clear.
* Write an informative paragraph.

Introduction Provide each student with a copy of the writing frame (page 30). Read the title and first line. Also draw attention to the illustration and labels. Ask students if they have ever used or seen a hammock. Tell them that they will write a paragraph explaining what a hammock is. Review that the purpose of informative writing is to tell the reader about the topic.

Model Use a think-aloud such as: *A paragraph is a group of sentences about the same idea or topic; often a paragraph begins with a sentence telling what the topic is.* Ask students to suggest a sentence to tell what a hammock is. For example:

* A hammock is a hanging bed used for sleeping or relaxing.

Tell students that a writer develops an informative paragraph by using facts and information to tell more about the topic. Invite students to make suggestions. For example:

* made of a strong material
* hung by cords or chains

* swings back and forth
* strung between two supports

Guide students in grouping their facts and information to help readers understand their explanation. For example, in the groups below, three facts tell what a hammock is like while one fact tells what a hammock does. Coach students in developing complete and more informative sentences to use in the paragraph. For example:

* A hammock is made of a strong material.
* It is hung by cords or chains.
* The cords are strung between two supports, such as trees.

* A hammock swings back and forth when you are in it.

Guided Practice Once you have developed a sample paragraph, have students complete the writing frame. Encourage them to use their own words and sentence structure when they group their ideas and write their paragraphs.

Review Invite volunteers to read their finished paragraphs to the class. Have listeners use items 1–4, 6, and 12 on the assessment checklist (page 63) to evaluate the effectiveness of other students' paragraphs.

Independent Practice Use the On Your Own activity (page 31) as homework or review. Encourage students to use what they learned in the lesson to complete it. Tell them they can choose a topic from the Idea Box or use their own idea. It may be helpful for students to draw a picture of their topic before writing about it.

Name _____ Date _____

Here's a Hammock

What is a hammock?

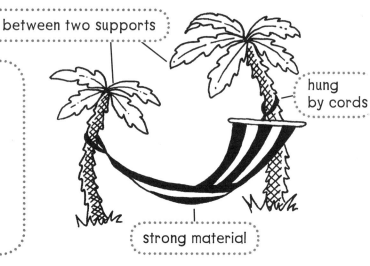

between two supports

hung by cords

strong material

- Introduce the topic by telling what a hammock is.
- Focus on your writing purpose.
- Write facts about the topic.
- Group the facts and information.
- Write your paragraph on another sheet of paper.

Topic _____

Writing Purpose _____

_____

Facts and Information _____

_____

_____

_____

_____

Group the Facts and Information

What a Hammock Is Like _____

_____

_____

_____

What a Hammock Does _____

_____

_____

_____

Name _____ Date _____

On Your Own

Choose a place to sleep from the Idea Box or think of your own idea. Complete the page. Then, write a paragraph on another sheet of paper to explain what the topic is.

Idea Box

○ Crib   ○ Sleeping Bag   ○ Bunk Beds   ○ My Idea:

_____

_____

Topic _____

Writing Purpose _____

_____

Facts and Information _____

_____

_____

_____

_____

Group the Facts and Information

What It Is Like _____

_____

_____

_____

What It Does _____

_____

_____

_____

Writing Lessons to Meet the Common Core: Grade 3 © 2013 by Linda Ward Beech, Scholastic Teaching Resources

Informative Writing
All About Pizza

Objectives & Common Core Connections

* Introduce the topic.
* Focus on the purpose of informative writing.
* Develop information about the topic.
* Use facts to tell about the topic.
* Group and organize information to make the topic clear.
* Use linking words to connect ideas.
* Write an informative paragraph.

Introduction Provide each student with a copy of the writing frame (page 33). Read the title and first line. Also draw attention to the illustration. Tell students that they will write a paragraph explaining what a pizza is. Remind them that the purpose of informative writing is to give information about a topic to the reader.

Model Review that a paragraph is a group of sentences about the same idea or topic; a paragraph has a sentence telling what its topic is. On the board, write a sentence to introduce the topic of pizza. For example:

* Pizza is a kind of food eaten by many people.

Remind students that the next sentences in a paragraph tell more about the topic. A writer can develop an informative paragraph by using facts and information about the topic. Stress that a fact is a statement that can be proved true or false; for example, you can prove that pizza is a food.

Ask students to suggest other facts about pizza that could be used to help explain what pizza is. For example:

* round pie
* dough crust
* tomato sauce
* cheese topping
* cut into slices
* eat with hands

Coach students in grouping their facts and information to best help the reader understand the information they are sharing. For example, the first group below describes pizza while the second group tells what to do with it. Point out how some facts can be connected using linking words, such as *and, another,* or *also*.

* Pizza is a round pie.
* It has a crust made of dough.
* Pizza also has tomato sauce on it and a cheese topping.

* You cut a pizza into slices to eat it.
* Another thing about pizza is that you can eat it with your hands.

Guided Practice Once you have developed a sample paragraph, have students complete the writing frame. Point out that they can use other facts to support the topic if they wish. Encourage students to use their own words and sentence structure when they group their ideas and write their paragraphs.

Review Invite volunteers to read their finished paragraphs to the class. Have listeners use items 1–4, 6, 7, and 12 on the assessment checklist (page 63) to evaluate the effectiveness of other students' paragraphs.

Independent Practice Use the On Your Own activity (page 34) as homework or review. Encourage students to use what they learned in the lesson to complete it. Explain that they can choose a food from the Idea Box or think of another food.

Name _____ Date _____

All About Pizza

What is a pizza?

- Introduce the topic.
- Focus on your writing purpose.
- Write facts about the topic.
- Group the facts and information.
- Use linking words.
- Write your paragraph on another sheet of paper.

Topic _____

Writing Purpose _____

_____

Facts and Information _____

_____

_____

_____

_____

Group the Facts and Information

What a Pizza Is _____

_____

_____

_____

What You Do With a Pizza _____

_____

_____

_____

_____

Linking Words _____

On Your Own

Choose a food topic from the Idea Box or think of another food. Complete the page. Then, write a paragraph on another sheet of paper to explain what the topic is.

Idea Box

○ Salad   ○ Sandwich   ○ Taco   ○ My Idea: _____
_____

Topic _____

Writing Purpose _____

_____

Facts and Information _____

_____

_____

_____

_____

Group the Facts and Information

Group 1 _____

_____

_____

Group 2 _____

_____

_____

_____

Linking Words _____

Writing Lessons to Meet the Common Core: Grade 3 © 2013 by Linda Ward Beech, Scholastic Teaching Resources

Explanatory Writing
Rain Gauge

Objectives & Common Core Connections

* Introduce the topic.
* Focus on the purpose of explanatory writing.
* List materials and steps.
* Organize steps in a logical order.
* Write an explanatory paragraph.

Introduction Provide each student with a copy of the writing frame (page 36). Read the title and first lines. Also have students study the illustration. Point out that an explanatory paragraph can tell how to make or do something. Explain that a rain gauge might be helpful if students were working on a science project. Tell students that they will write a paragraph telling how to make a rain gauge.

Model Help students begin their explanation by writing an introductory sentence. For example:

* You can make a rain gauge to measure rainfall.

Tell students that when explaining how to make something, they will need to list materials and steps. For example:

* collect a tall plastic glass, a six-inch ruler, tape
* attach ruler to glass
* put gauge outside when rain is predicted
* check gauge when rain stops

Point out that the steps must be given in a logical order so someone can follow them. Coach students in developing complete and more informative sentences to use in a paragraph. For example:

* Collect a tall plastic glass, a six-inch ruler, and tape.
* Tape the ruler to the side of the glass so the one-inch mark is at the bottom.
* When rain is predicted, set the rain gauge outside, away from buildings and trees.
* When the rain stops, check the gauge to measure the rainfall.

Guided Practice Once you have developed a sample paragraph, have students complete the writing frame. Encourage them to use their own words and sentence structure.

Review Invite volunteers to read their finished paragraphs to the class. Have listeners use items 1, 2, 8, 9, and 12 on the assessment checklist (page 63) to evaluate the effectiveness of other students' paragraphs.

Independent Practice Use the On Your Own activity (page 37) as homework or review. Encourage students to use what they learned in the lesson to complete the it. Tell them they can choose a science topic from the Idea Box or use their own idea. Point out that students may need to do some research. Have science textbooks or similar resources available.

Name _____ Date _____

Rain Gauge

A rain gauge measures rainfall.
You can make a rain gauge to find out
how much rain falls in your neighborhood.

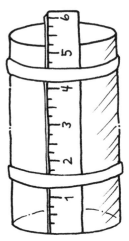

- Introduce the topic.
- Focus on your writing purpose.
- List the materials and steps.
- Put the steps in order.
- Write your paragraph on another sheet of paper.

Topic _____

_____

Writing Purpose _____

_____

Materials _____   Steps _____

_____   _____

_____   _____

_____   _____

Steps in Order _____

_____

_____

_____

_____

Name _____ Date _____

On Your Own

Choose a science topic from the Idea Box or think of one of your own. Complete the page. Then, write your paragraph on another sheet of paper to explain how to make or do something.

Idea Box

○ How to make shadow pictures

○ How to make a needle compass

○ How to grow a plant from an avocado pit

○ My Idea: _____

_____

Topic _____

_____

Writing Purpose _____

_____

Materials _____   Steps _____

_____   _____

_____   _____

_____   _____

_____   _____

Steps in Order _____

_____

_____

_____

_____

_____

Explanatory Writing
Fan Fun

Objectives & Common Core Connections

✳ Introduce the topic.

✳ Focus on the purpose of explanatory writing.

✳ List materials and steps.

✳ Organize steps in a logical order.

✳ Include an illustration.

✳ Write an explanatory paragraph.

Introduction Provide each student with a copy of the writing frame (page 39). Have students read the title and first line. Then, discuss the illustrations. Point out that an explanatory paragraph can tell how to do something. Tell students that they will write a paragraph explaining how to make a paper fan.

Model Help students begin their explanation by writing an introductory sentence. For example:

• It is easy to make a paper fan.

Share with students that when explaining how to make something, they will need to list materials and steps. Ask what materials and steps would be needed to make a fan. For example:

• collect paper, tape, crayons

• fold the paper in pleats

• fasten the bottom with tape

• decorate the paper with crayons

Point out that the steps must be listed in a logical order so someone can follow them.

Coach students in arranging the steps so they follow a logical order (and in using transitional words, such as *first, next, then,* and *finally,* or *last* to indicate sequence). Point out that it would be difficult to decorate the paper once it has been folded and fastened so decorating the paper should be the second step. Model how to develop complete and more informative sentences to use in a paragraph. For example:

• <u>First</u>, collect paper, tape, and crayons.

• <u>Next</u>, decorate the paper in a colorful design.

• <u>Then</u>, fold the paper into pleats.

• <u>Last</u>, fasten the bottom of the pleated paper with tape to make a fan shape.

Mention that it is helpful to include an illustration to aid the reader with certain explanations. Talk with students about how the illustrations on the writing frame help a reader know what to do.

Guided Practice Once you have developed a sample paragraph, have students complete the writing frame. Encourage them to use their own words and sentence structure.

Review Invite volunteers to read their finished paragraphs to the class. Have listeners use items 1, 2, 8–10, and 12 on the assessment checklist (page 63) to evaluate the effectiveness of other students' paragraphs.

Independent Practice Use the On Your Own activity (page 40) as homework or review. Encourage students to use what they learned in the lesson to complete it. Tell them they can choose a topic from the Idea Box or use their own idea.

Fan Fun

How can you make a fan?

- Introduce the topic.
- Focus on your writing purpose.
- List the materials and steps.
- Put the steps in order.
- Write your paragraph on a separate sheet of paper.

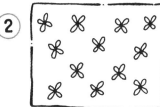

Topic _____

_____

Writing Purpose _____

_____

Materials _____   Steps _____

_____   _____

_____   _____

_____   _____

Steps in Order _____

_____

_____

_____

_____

_____

_____

On Your Own

Choose an item you can make from paper from the Idea Box or think of your own idea. Complete the page. Then, on separate sheets of paper, write a paragraph and draw a picture to explain how to make something from paper.

Idea Box

○ glider   ○ chain   ○ hat   ○ My Idea:

_____

_____

Topic _____

_____

Writing Purpose _____

_____

Materials _____   Steps _____

_____   _____

_____   _____

_____   _____

_____   _____

Steps in Order _____

_____

_____

_____

_____

_____

Writing Lessons to Meet the Common Core: Grade 3 © 2013 by Linda Ward Beech, Scholastic Teaching Resources

Informative Writing
In the Animal World

Introduction Provide each student with a copy of the writing frame (page 42). Have students read the title and first line. Also discuss the illustration. Tell them that they will write a paragraph explaining what a walrus is. Remind students that it is often necessary to do research to write an informative paragraph.

Model Help students begin their informative paragraph by writing an introductory sentence using facts and details. For example:

* A walrus is a large sea animal that lives in icy Arctic waters.

Ask students to think of or find other facts and information that helps tell a reader what a walrus is. For example:

* long tusks
* good swimmer
* thick skin
* four flippers
* whiskers

Coach students in developing complete sentences with more details to use in a paragraph. Model how some ideas can be connected with linking words. For example:

* A walrus has thick, wrinkled skin. It has long teeth called tusks that it uses for defense and whiskers that help it find food. A walrus also has four flippers that help make it a good swimmer.

Tell students that a good informative paragraph usually has a concluding sentence. This sentence restates or summarizes information in the paragraph. For example:

* The features of a walrus help it survive in its cold environment.

Guided Practice Once you have developed a sample paragraph, have students complete the writing frame. Encourage them to use their own wording and sentence structure as well as other information that they know or have researched about walruses.

Review Invite volunteers to read their finished paragraphs to the class. Have listeners use items 1–7, 11, and 12 on the assessment checklist (page 63) to evaluate the effectiveness of other students' paragraphs.

Independent Practice Use the On Your Own activity (page 43) as homework or review. Encourage students to use what they learned in the lesson to complete it. Tell them that they can choose a topic from the Idea Box or think of another animal. Remind students that they will most likely have to do some research to find facts and details for their topic. If possible, have appropriate books or a computer with Internet access available for student research.

In the Animal World

What is a walrus?

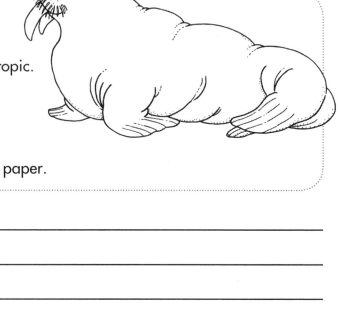

- Introduce the topic.
- Focus on your writing purpose.
- Find and write facts and details about the topic.
- List linking words you might use.
- Write practice sentences.
- Provide a concluding sentence.
- Write your paragraph on another sheet of paper.

Topic _____

Writing Purpose _____

Facts and Details _____

_____

_____

_____

_____

Linking Words _____

_____

Practice Sentences _____

_____

_____

_____

_____

Concluding Sentence _____

_____

Writing Lessons to Meet the Common Core: Grade 3 © 2013 by Linda Ward Beech, Scholastic Teaching Resources

Name _____ Date _____

On Your Own

Choose an animal from the Idea Box or think of one of your own. Find facts and details about the animal. Complete this page. Then, write a paragraph on another sheet of paper that tells what the animal is like.

Idea Box

○ Penguin　　○ Camel　　○ Kangaroo　　○ My Idea:

_____
_____

Topic _____

Writing Purpose _____

Facts and Details _____

_____

_____

_____

_____

Linking Words _____

_____

Sentences _____

_____

_____

_____

_____

_____

Concluding Sentence _____

_____

Narrative Writing
Imagine That

Objectives & Common Core Connections

* Develop a real or imagined experience or event.
* Focus on the purpose of narrative writing.
* Establish the situation and characters.
* Write a good opening sentence.

Introduction Provide each student with a copy of the writing frame (page 45). Have students read the title and first line. Also discuss the illustration. Ask students what story they think it suggests. Talk about whether the story is real or imagined. Explain to students that they will be developing a narrative about the picture. Remind them that a narrative is a story or account of something and is usually written to entertain the reader.

Model Summarize the situation suggested by the illustration. You might say: *The illustration shows a mysterious paw reaching for the girl's carrot.*

Suggest a sentence to begin a narrative about the situation. Remind students that a story needs a good beginning so that the reader will want to continue. For example:

* Slowly and quietly, the huge furry paw reached toward the carrot.

Continue by talking about the girl in the illustration. You might say: *I need to give the girl a name and tell something about her.* Invite students to contribute their ideas. For example:

* The girl's name is Patty. She's about nine, and she's pretty brave. She doesn't know the paw is there, but she's not the kind of girl to give up her carrot easily.

Invite volunteers to describe the paw. Ask questions such as: *Does it belong to an animal? A make-believe creature? What is this character like?* Students might say:

* The paw belongs to a young monster. His name is Perkins. He is hungry because he got lost from his monster family and has no one to cook dinner for him. Maybe Patty will help him.

Guided Practice Have students complete the writing frame. Encourage them to use their own ideas about the story situation and characters. Suggest that students use another sheet of paper to illustrate the characters in their narrative.

Review Invite volunteers to share their finished pages with the class. Have listeners use items 1–5 on the assessment checklist (page 64) to evaluate the effectiveness of other students' work.

Independent Practice Use the On Your Own activity (page 46) as homework or review. Tell students to use what they learned in the lesson to complete the page. Explain that they can choose a topic from the Idea Box or use their own idea. Encourage students to include at least two characters and provide a description and background information for each.

Imagine That

⭐ Use the picture to tell a story.

- Focus on your writing purpose.
- Tell what is happening.
- Describe the characters.
- Begin with a good opening sentence.

Writing Purpose _____

_____

What Is Happening _____

_____

_____

_____

_____

_____

Character 1 _____

_____

_____

Character 2 _____

_____

_____

Opening Sentence _____

_____

Name _____ Date _____

On Your Own

Choose a story topic from the Idea Box or think of one of your own. Complete this page. Draw a picture to go with your story ideas on another sheet of paper.

Idea Box

○ Prince Who Likes Being a Frog   ○ My Idea: _____

○ Girl's Desk Is a Spaceship   _____

○ Boy Steps Into a Painting   _____

_____

Writing Purpose _____

_____

What Is Happening _____

_____

_____

_____

_____

_____

Character 1 _____

_____

_____

Character 2 _____

_____

_____

Opening Sentence _____

_____

Narrative Writing
Going Away

Objectives & Common Core Connections

✳ Develop a real or imagined experience or event.

✳ Focus on the purpose of narrative writing.

✳ Establish a situation and characters.

✳ Write a good opening sentence.

✳ Organize a clear event sequence.

✳ Use temporal words to signal event order.

Introduction Provide each student with a copy of the writing frame (page 48). Have students read the title and first line. Also discuss the illustrations. Tell students they will be developing a narrative about the illustrations. Review that a narrative is a story or account of something that is written to entertain the reader.

Model Summarize the situation suggested by the illustrations. You might say: *A girl is packing her clothes to go somewhere, and at the last moment she packs her stuffed bunny.* Discuss how the girl and the bunny might be characters in this narrative. Encourage students to give each character a name and feelings. Ask students to think about why the girl packs the bunny.

Model a sentence to begin a narrative about the situation. For example:

- It was time to pack for a sleepover at her friend's house, and Tina was nervous.

Then, describe what the pictures show. For example:

- gets out suitcase and clothes
- adds a stuffed bunny
- checks she has everything she needs
- puts her clothes in the suitcase

Ask students what they notice about this sequence of events (*out of order*). Remind them that a narrative has a beginning, middle, and end. Have them describe the correct sequence of the girl's actions. Then, work with students to develop complete and more informative sentences to tell the sequence. Model how sequence can be made clear by the use of time words. For example:

- Tina got her suitcase from under the bed and the clothes she would need from the dresser. <u>Then</u>, she packed the clothes in the suitcase. Did Tina have everything she needed? <u>At the last minute</u>, she put Fluffy into the suitcase, too. Taking Fluffy along made her feel better.

Guided Practice Have students complete the writing frame. Encourage them to use their own ideas about the story situation and characters. For example, suggest that students think about how Fluffy might feel (*possibly sad at first about being left behind and then happy*).

Review Invite volunteers to share their finished pages with the class. Have listeners use items 1–7 on the assessment checklist (page 64) to evaluate the effectiveness of other students' work.

Independent Practice Use the On Your Own activity (page 49) as homework or review. Tell students to use what they learned in the lesson to complete the page. Explain that they can choose a topic from the Idea Box or use one of their own. Encourage students to include at least two characters and provide information about the feelings of each.

Name _____ Date _____

Going Away

Use the pictures to tell a story.

- Focus on your writing purpose.
- Tell what is happening.
- Describe the characters.
- Begin with a good opening sentence.
- Organize events in order.
- Use time words.

Writing Purpose _____

What Is Happening _____

_____

_____

_____

Character 1 _____

_____

Character 2 _____

_____

Opening Sentence _____

_____

Order of Events _____

_____

_____

_____

_____

_____

Time Words _____

Writing Lessons to Meet the Common Core: Grade 3 © 2013 by Linda Ward Beech, Scholastic Teaching Resources

On Your Own

Choose a story topic from the Idea Box or think of one of your own. Complete this page. Draw pictures to go with your story ideas on a separate sheet of paper.

Idea Box

○ A Runaway Pet's Adventure

○ Boy Enters a Sandcastle-Building Contest

○ Girl Finds a Time Machine

○ My Idea: _____

_____

_____

Writing Purpose _____

What Is Happening _____

_____

_____

_____

Character 1 _____

_____

Character 2 _____

_____

Opening Sentence _____

_____

Order of Events _____

_____

_____

_____

_____

_____

Time Words _____

Narrative Writing
Silly Sock Story

Objectives & Common Core Connections

* Develop a real or imagined experience or event.
* Focus on the purpose of narrative writing.
* Establish a situation and characters.
* Organize a clear event sequence.
* Use dialogue to show characters' responses.
* Write a narrative.

Introduction Provide each student with a copy of the writing frame (page 51). Ask students to read the title and first lines. Also discuss the illustrations. Explain that students will develop dialogue for a narrative about the pictures. Review that a narrative is written to entertain the reader.

Model Summarize the situation suggested by the illustrations. You might say: *The man must have bought two different socks instead of a matching pair. He seems angry, and the clerk seems surprised.*

Help students develop events for a story. Remind them that the events should be in a logical sequence. For example:

* Man buys socks and finds they don't match.
* Man calls clerk at the store.
* Man returns to the store.
* Man decides to keep the socks.

Model for students what the characters might be saying on the phone. For example:

Man: You sold me socks that don't match! I want my money back.

Clerk: That's impossible! All our socks come in matching pairs.

Man: I'm bringing these socks back.

Invite students to suggest what the man and clerk say when the customer returns to the store. For example:

Man: This is an outrage! How am I supposed to wear these?

Clerk: Maybe you could make puppets from them.

Man: Wow! That's a great idea! Do you have any more pairs like this?

Clerk: I think you got the only pair.

Guided Practice Have students complete the writing frame. Encourage them to use their own ideas for dialogue.

Review Invite volunteers to share their finished pages with the class. Have listeners use items 1–4, 6, 8, and 11 on the assessment checklist (page 64) to evaluate the effectiveness of other students' work.

Independent Practice Use the On Your Own activity (page 52) as homework or review. Tell students to use what they learned in the lesson to complete it. Explain that they can choose a topic from the Idea Box or use one of their own. Encourage students to include at least two characters and suggest that they title their finished narratives.

Name _____   Date _____

Silly Sock Story

⭐ What does the man say?
⠇ What does the sales clerk say?

- Focus on your writing purpose.
- Tell what is happening and who the characters are.
- Organize events in order.
- Use dialogue to make the story clear.
- Write your narrative on another sheet of paper.

Writing Purpose _____

What Is Happening _____

_____

_____

Character 1 _____   Character 2 _____

Order of Events _____

_____

_____

_____

Dialogue _____

_____

_____

_____

_____

_____

_____

Name _____ Date _____

On Your Own

Choose a story topic from the Idea Box or think of one of your own. Complete this page. Then, write your narrative on another sheet of paper.

Idea Box

○ Truck Driver Scolds Jaywalker

○ Small Boy Borrows Older Brother's Bicycle

○ Two Hikers Discuss Which Fork in Trail to Take

○ My Idea: _____

_____

Writing Purpose _____

What Is Happening _____

_____

_____

Character 1 _____ Character 2 _____

Order of Events _____

_____

_____

_____

Dialogue _____

_____

_____

_____

_____

_____

Writing Lessons to Meet the Common Core: Grade 3 © 2013 by Linda Ward Beech, Scholastic Teaching Resources

Narrative Writing
Flying Power

Objectives & Common Core Connections

* Develop a real or imagined experience or event.
* Focus on the purpose of narrative writing.
* Establish a situation and characters.
* Organize a clear event sequence.
* Use dialogue to show characters' responses.
* Add descriptive details to develop events.
* Write a narrative.

Introduction Provide each student with a copy of the writing frame (page 54). Ask students to read the title and first line. Also discuss the illustration. Explain that students will write descriptive details for a narrative about the picture.

Model Summarize the situation suggested by the illustration. You might say: *The boy and girl are flying, maybe to help the cat.*

Begin by developing sentences with dialogue about the situation and characters. For example:

* Asher and Kim were walking home from school when they heard a cat. "Yeooow!" Its terrified cries came from high in a nearby tree.
* "I wish we could fly up there and help that cat," said Kim.

Next, help students develop events for a story. For example:

* kids flap arms
* suddenly they are in the air flying
* they rescue cat

* they return cat to ground
* their flying power disappears

Model sentences to show how descriptive details can make events and feelings more vivid. For example:

* Just for fun, the kids flapped their arms like birds.
* Suddenly, they were really flying, soaring in the cool, clear air.
* They fluttered close to the tree branch, and Kim slipped the frightened cat onto Asher's back.
* Carefully, they flew to a bench on the ground and let the cat go.
* When they tried to lift off again, Kim and Asher found their flying power was gone. It was only for doing good deeds.

Guided Practice Have students complete the writing frame. Encourage them to use their own dialogue and details to describe the events.

Review Invite volunteers to share their finished pages with the class. Have listeners use items 1–4, 6, 8, 9, and 11 on the assessment checklist (page 64) to evaluate the effectiveness of other students' work.

Independent Practice Use the On Your Own activity (page 55) as homework or review. Encourage students to use what they learned in the lesson to complete it. Explain that they can choose a topic from the Idea Box or use one of their own. Suggest that students limit the number of characters to two or three. You might also invite them to title their finished narratives.

Name _____ Date _____

Flying Power

What is happening?

- Focus on your writing purpose.
- Tell what is happening.
- Tell who the characters are and what they say.
- Organize events in order.
- Use descriptive details to develop the events.
- Write your narrative on another sheet of paper.

Writing Purpose _____

What Is Happening _____

_____

_____

Character 1   Character 2   Character 3

_____   _____   _____

Dialogue _____

_____

_____

_____

Order of Events _____

_____

_____

_____

_____

Details _____

_____

Writing Lessons to Meet the Common Core: Grade 3 © 2013 by Linda Ward Beech, Scholastic Teaching Resources

Name _____ Date _____

On Your Own

Choose a story topic from the Idea Box or think of one of your own. Complete this page. Then, write your narrative on another sheet of paper.

Idea Box

○ Girl Lives in a Treehouse   ○ My Idea: _____

○ Boy Has a Talking Robot   _____

○ Dog Is Invisible for a Day   _____

Writing Purpose _____

What Is Happening _____

_____

_____

Character 1   Character 2

_____   _____   _____

Dialogue _____

_____

_____

_____

Order of Events _____

_____

_____

_____

_____

_____

Details _____

_____

_____

_____

Narrative Writing
At Sea

Objectives & Common Core Connections

* Develop a real or imagined experience or event.
* Focus on the purpose of narrative writing.
* Develop a good opening sentence.
* Establish a situation and characters.
* Organize a clear event sequence.
* Use dialogue to show characters' responses.
* Add descriptive details to develop events.
* Write a narrative.

Introduction Provide each student with a copy of the writing frame (page 57). Read the title and first line. Also discuss the illustration and point out the blank speech balloons. Explain that students will develop a narrative that includes dialogue and details.

Model Summarize the situation suggested by the illustration. You might say: *Some passengers aboard a cruise ship are reacting to the storm.* Work with students to develop opening sentences about the situation and characters. For example:

* A fierce storm tossed the ship through the waves over and over again. Mrs. Pardi clung to her husband as the ship heaved.

Lead students in developing a sequence of events. For example:

* ship is caught in storm
* the Pardis are upset
* ship finally docks
* the Pardis decide to spend vacation on land

Model sentences with dialogue to show how the characters might respond to the storm. For example:

* "What a horrible vacation!" sobbed Mrs. Pardi.
* "Don't worry," Dr. Pardi said. "The crew is used to storms."

Model sentences in which descriptive details show how the characters respond to the storm. For example:

* Although he spoke calmly, Dr. Pardi was biting his nails. Mrs. Pardi closed her eyes as if to make the storm disappear. When the storm let up and the ship docked, the couple rushed off carrying their suitcases. They planned to spend the rest of their vacation on land.

Guided Practice Have students complete the writing frame. Encourage them to use their own dialogue and details to show how the characters respond to the events.

Review Invite volunteers to share their finished pages with the class. Have listeners use items 1–6, 8, 9, and 11 on the assessment checklist (page 64) to evaluate the effectiveness of other students' work.

Independent Practice Use the On Your Own activity (page 58) as homework or review. Encourage students to use what they learned in the lesson to complete it. Explain that they can choose a topic from the Idea Box or use one of their own. Suggest that students limit the number of characters to two or three. You might also invite them to title their finished narratives.

At Sea

What's the story?

- Focus on your writing purpose.
- Tell what is happening and who the characters are.
- Write a good opening sentence.
- Organize events in order.
- Use dialogue and details to show how the characters respond to events.
- Write your narrative on another sheet of paper.

Writing Purpose _____

What Is Happening _____

_____

_____

Character 1   Character 2

_____   _____

Opening Sentence _____

_____

Order of Events _____

_____

_____

_____

_____

Dialogue and Details _____

_____

_____

_____

_____

Name _____ Date _____

On Your Own

Choose a story topic from the Idea Box or think of one of your own. Complete this page. Then, write your narrative on another sheet of paper.

Idea Box

○ Boy Misses the Bus for School   ○ My Idea: _____

○ Woman Gets on the Wrong Train   _____

○ Family Is Caught in Huge Traffic Jam   _____

Writing Purpose _____

What Is Happening _____

_____

_____

Character 1   Character 2

_____   _____

Opening Sentence _____

_____

Order of Events _____

_____

_____

_____

_____

Dialogue and Details _____

_____

_____

_____

_____

Narrative Writing
Snow Picture

* Develop a real or imagined experience or event.
* Focus on the purpose of narrative writing.
* Establish a situation and characters.
* Write a good opening sentence.
* Organize a clear event sequence.
* Use dialogue to show characters' responses.
* Add descriptive details to develop events.
* Provide a sense of closure.
* Write a narrative.

Introduction Provide each student with a copy of the writing frame (page 60). Read the title and first lines. Also discuss the illustration and point out the blank speech balloons. Explain that students will develop a narrative about the scene.

Model Summarize the situation suggested by the illustration. You might say: *It's night, and two children are watching a big snowstorm through the window.* Develop opening sentences. For example:

* The snow came down thick and fast, covering the houses, trees, bushes, and street. Ellen and Jake were excited.

Guide students in developing a sequence of events. For example:

* big snowstorm at night
* Ellen and Jake make snowman in morning
* Ellen gets upset when snowman melts that afternoon
* Jake comforts her with photo of snowman

Model sentences to show how the characters might respond to the snow. For example:

* "I'm going to make a snowman," Jake said.
* "Me, too!" Ellen cried.

Model sentences in which descriptive details show how the characters respond to the snow. For example:

* Ellen and Jake worked hard, building a glistening snowman with a long turnip nose. They named him Jolly because he made them happy. However, by afternoon the sun was melting Jolly. He looked worn and sad. Ellen ran into the house crying.

Point out that a narrative has an ending or conclusion. Give as an example:

* Jake followed her. "Jolly isn't gone," he said, and handed her a photograph he had taken of the snowman earlier that morning.

Guided Practice Have students complete the writing frame. Encourage them to use their own dialogue, details, and ending.

Review Invite volunteers to share their finished pages with the class. Have listeners use items 1–6 and 8–11 on the assessment checklist (page 64) to evaluate the effectiveness of other students' work.

Independent Practice Use the On Your Own activity (page 61) as homework or review. Encourage students to use what they learned in the lesson to complete it. Explain that they can choose a topic from the Idea Box or use one of their own. Suggest that students limit the number of characters to two or three. You might also invite them to title their finished narratives.

Snow Picture

It's a snowy night. What will happen tomorrow?

- Focus on your writing purpose.
- Tell what is happening and who the characters are.
- Organize events in order.
- Use dialogue and details to show how characters respond to events.
- Provide a good opening sentence and an ending to the story.
- Write your narrative on another sheet of paper.

Writing Purpose _____

What Is Happening _____

_____

Character 1 _____ Character 2 _____

Opening Sentence _____

_____

Order of Events _____

_____

_____

_____

Dialogue and Details _____

_____

_____

_____

_____

Ending _____

_____

On Your Own

Choose a story topic from the Idea Box or think of one of your own. Complete this page. Then, write your narrative on another sheet of paper.

Idea Box

○ Shy Child Gets Lead in School Play   ○ My Idea: _____

○ Identical Twins Confuse Neighbors   _____

○ Storm Knocks Out Electricity   _____

Writing Purpose _____

What Is Happening _____

_____

Character 1   Character 2   Character 3

_____   _____   _____

Opening Sentence _____

_____

Order of Events _____

_____

_____

_____

Dialogue and Details _____

_____

_____

_____

_____

Ending _____

Name _____ Date _____

Student Assessment Checklist
Opinion Writing

1. Introduced the topic. .... ☐

2. Focused on the writing purpose. .... ☐

3. Stated an opinion. .... ☐

4. Developed and presented reasons to support an opinion. .... ☐

5. Wrote sentences that include reasons for the opinion. .... ☐

6. Connected the reasons and opinion with linking words. .... ☐

7. Provided a concluding sentence. .... ☐

8. Wrote a paragraph that offers an opinion. .... ☐

More Things to Check

● Capitalized proper nouns. ☐

● Capitalized the first word of sentences. ☐

● Used correct punctuation. ☐

● Spelled words correctly. ☐

● Followed correct paragraph form. ☐

Writing Lessons to Meet the Common Core: Grade 3 © 2013 by Linda Ward Beech, Scholastic Teaching Resources

Name _____ Date _____

Student Assessment Checklist
Informative/Explanatory Writing

1. Introduced and/or defined the topic. .... ☐

2. Focused on the writing purpose. .... ☐

3. Developed information about the topic. .... ☐

4. Used facts to tell about the topic. .... ☐

5. Developed the topic with details. .... ☐

6. Grouped facts and information to make the topic clear. .... ☐

7. Used linking words to connect ideas. .... ☐

8. Listed the materials and steps. .... ☐

9. Organized steps in order. .... ☐

10. Included an illustration to aid comprehension. .... ☐

11. Provided a concluding sentence. .... ☐

12. Wrote an informative/explanatory paragraph. .... ☐

More Things to Check

● Capitalized proper nouns. ☐

● Capitalized the first word of sentences. ☐

● Used correct punctuation. ☐

● Spelled words correctly. ☐

● Followed correct paragraph form. ☐

Student Assessment Checklist
Narrative Writing

1. Developed a real or imagined experience or event. .... ☐

2. Focused on the writing purpose. .... ☐

3. Established a situation. .... ☐

4. Established characters. .... ☐

5. Developed a good opening sentence. .... ☐

6. Organized events in sequence. .... ☐

7. Used time words to signal event order. .... ☐

8. Included dialogue. .... ☐

9. Used descriptive details. .... ☐

10. Provided a conclusion. .... ☐

11. Wrote a narrative. .... ☐

More Things to Check

● Capitalized proper nouns. ☐

● Capitalized the first word of sentences. ☐

● Used correct punctuation. ☐

● Spelled words correctly. ☐

● Followed correct paragraph form. ☐

Writing Lessons to Meet the Common Core: Grade 3 © 2013 by Linda Ward Beech, Scholastic Teaching Resources